# 20-MINUTE (OR LESS)
# FILTER
# HACKS

**SHEELA PREUITT**

Lerner Publications ◆ Minneapolis

Mom and Dad, thanks for your steadfast support in all my endeavors.

# Online Safety

Children should always ask permission before going online, especially when using a new website. Stay safe online by protecting your identity. Never share personal information such as your full name, address, or email address online. Think carefully about posting personal photos of yourself, and don't post pictures of friends or family without permission.

Lerner Publications Company
An imprint of Lerner Publishing Group, Inc.
241 First Avenue North
Minneapolis, MN 55401 USA

For reading levels and more information, look up this title at www.lernerbooks.com

Main body text set in Conduit ITC Std Regular 13/17
Typeface provided by ITC

**Library of Congress Cataloging-in-Publication Data**
Names: Preuitt, Sheela, author.
Title: 20-minute (or less) filter hacks / Sheela Preuitt.
Other titles: Twenty minute (or less) filter hacks
Description: Minneapolis : Lerner Publications, 2020. | Series: Vidcode coding hacks | Includes index. | Audience: Ages 8–12. | Audience: Grades 4–6. | Summary: "Create a filter, dress up a photo! Readers will learn solid coding skills while they build their own filters using the book's instructions and projects on the Vidcode platform"— Provided by publisher.
Identifiers: LCCN 2019052539 (print) | LCCN 2019052540 (ebook) | ISBN 9781541597181 (library binding) | ISBN 9781728401430 (ebook)
Subjects: LCSH: Image processing—Digital techniques—Juvenile literature. | Digital filters (Mathematics)—Juvenile literature.
Classification: LCC TA1637 .P74 2020 (print) | LCC TA1637 (ebook) | DDC 006.6/96—dc23

LC record available at https://lccn.loc.gov/2019052539
LC ebook record available at https://lccn.loc.gov/2019052540

Manufactured in the United States of America
1 – CG – 7/15/20

# TABLE OF CONTENTS

# CODE YOUR VIDEO FILTERS

Have you ever wondered how to get an artistic and unique look for your pictures and videos? You can do it in 20 minutes or less with filters! Filters are small computer **programs** that change photos or videos. Using the Vidcode platform, you can add fun filters with just a few lines of code. You'll be programming before you know it!

**Coding** takes practice. As you learn, you might give the computer a wrong instruction and end up with something you don't like. When this happens, don't worry! Stop, think, and change your code to get the result you want.

Ready to show off your creativity?

To complete each project in this book, you can work online at the Vidcode Lerner sandbox. You will be able to save and customize your personal projects.

vidcode

**GO HERE TO GET STARTED!**

qrs.lernerbooks.com/
Filters

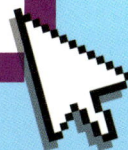

# CREATE A FILTER

JavaScript is a **programming language**. Use JavaScript to tell a computer what to do and become a programmer!

## CODING SKILLS

- functions
- arguments

6

Click the Back and Next buttons in the instruction panel at any time to unlock effects and access useful tips and tricks.

1. Upload your own video clip or click on a video from the Backgrounds tab. The video will appear as two lines of code in the **code editor**.

2. From the Effects tab, drag and drop the tint block into the code editor. Tint is a JavaScript **function**. A function does a specific task.

3. The code editor now shows `tint("red", 50)`. The **values** red and 50 are function **arguments**. They offer more information about the function task.

4. Watch your video. Did it turn red? Congratulations! You have written your first program.

**1**

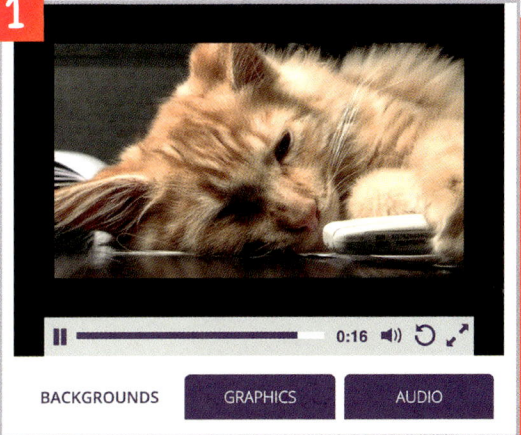

BACKGROUNDS    GRAPHICS    AUDIO

**3**

```
1 movie = video();
2 movie.source = "sleepy_cat.mp4";
3
4 tint("red", 50);
```

## CODING TIP!

Click on "red" in the code editor to see a popup color picker that lets you customize your tint color!

# RECREATE A FILTER

Computers perform instructions in order, from top to bottom. Change the order of your code and see what happens!

PROJECT TIME:
15 MINUTES

## CODING SKILLS

- data types
- strings
- numbers

1. Click on the dinosaur video.

2. Drag the tint block from Effects into the code editor. Click anywhere within the line of code. Replace the word "red" with "yellow." The code should now read (`"yellow"`, `50`). What happens to the video?

3. Now drag the grayscale block into the code editor.

```
1  movie = video();
2  movie.source = "dinosaur.mp4";
3
4  tint("yellow", 50);
5  grayscale();
```

4. Watch the video. Does the result match the prehistoric filter shown in the Instructions panel? Delete the code and repeat steps 1 through 3, but this time drag grayscale first. How does that change the result?

5. Did the order of functions matter? (Yes! This is called **sequence**!)

## HACK IT!

In the function tint(`"yellow"`, `50`); "yellow" and 50 are both arguments. Every argument has a type. Quotation marks indicate that "yellow" is a **string**. And 50 is a number. Strings and numbers are different **data types**. Many different data types are used when coding with JavaScript.

# DIGITAL QUILT

**PROJECT TIME:** 10 MINUTES

Create a unique filter using the "pixelate" function. Just like a quilt is made of different fabrics, your digital quilt will be made of blocks of colored **pixels**!

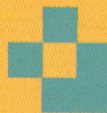

## CODING SKILLS
- functions
- values

1. Click on a video in Backgrounds.

2. From Effects, drag the pixelate block and drop it into the code editor. Your video now displays as square blocks of color.

3. Drag and drop other functions from Effects. Watch what happens to the video as you stack multiple functions.

4. Delete the code and repeat steps 1 through 3. Change the order in which you add functions until you create something you love!

**3**

```
1 movie = video();
2 movie.source = "lights.mp4";
3
4 pixelate(50);
5
6 color_invert();
7 vignette(50);
8 noise(50);
```

**CODING TIP!**

Adjust the value of a function by clicking on its line of code and changing the number. Watch how changing these values changes your digital quilt.

**4**

```
1 movie = video();
2 movie.source = "lights.mp4";
3
4 pixelate(50);
5
6 noise(50);
7 vignette(50);
8 color_invert();
```

# STAINED GLASS FILTER

Create rectangular **objects** and name them using a **variable**.
Then alter these rectangles by referencing their variables!

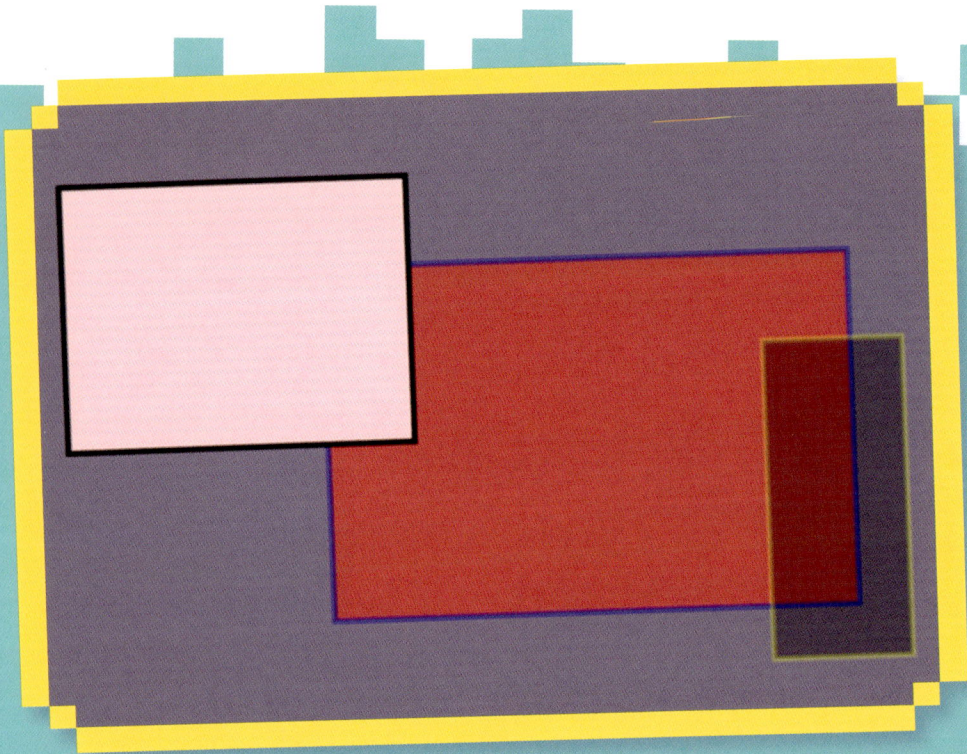

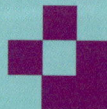

## CODING SKILLS

- objects
- variables

**1.** Drag and drop a rectangle block from Effects into the code editor.

**2.** The code editor now shows:
`var my_rect = rect(0, 0, 150, 200);`
The code `var` stands for variable. And `my_rect` is the name of your variable!

**3.** Click in the line of code. Change the name of your rectangle from `my_rect` to `container1`.

**4.** The function `rect(0, 0, 150, 200);` has four arguments. The first and second refer to the 'x' and 'y' position of the top left corner of the rectangle. The third argument is the rectangle's width, and the fourth argument is the rectangle's height. Click in the code and change these numbers. Watch how the position and size of the rectangle changes too!

**1**

| Instructions | 1 / 11 ▾ |

**Adding rectangles**

In order to help the facts in your PSA stand out, you can customize a rectangle to go behind them. In this tutorial, you'll review how to customize rectangles and squares!

**To start, drag the 'rectangle' button below into your code editor.**

**NEXT →**

EFFECTS    REFERENCE

rectangle

**4**

```
1
2 var container1 = rect(200, 100, 300, 200);
```

13

**5.** Size is just one thing you can change. You can also change the color, border color, and **opacity** of your rectangles. Type the following **properties** in the code editor under the main line of code:

```
container1.color = "red";
container1.opacity = 0.5;
container1.borderColor = "blue";
```

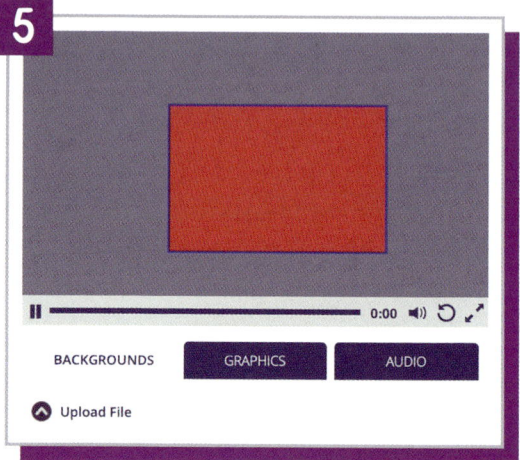

**6.** Add two more rectangles. Repeat step 3 to name the new rectangles `container2` and `container3`.

```
2  var container1 = rect(200, 100, 300, 200);
3
4  container1.color = "red";
5  container1.opacity =0.5;
6  container1.borderColor = "blue";
7
8  var container2 = rect(0, 0, 150, 200);
9  var container3 = rect(0, 0, 150, 200);
```

**7.** Repeat steps 4 and 5 to change the size, colors, and opacity of `container2` and `container3`. The opacity value can only be between 0 and 1. Play around with all values until you create a digital work of art that resembles stained glass!

```
2  var container1 = rect(200, 100, 300, 200);
3
4  container1.color = "red";
5  container1.opacity = 0.5;
6  container1.borderColor = "blue";
7
8  var container2 = rect(50, 50, 200, 150);
9
10 container2.color = "pink";
11 container2.opacity = 1;
12 container2.borderColor = "black";
13
14 var container3 = rect(450, 150, 80, 180);
15
16 container3.color = "black";
17 container3.opacity = 0.3;
18 container3.borderColor = "yellow";
19
20
```

## CODING TIP!

Variables are key to writing programs. Variables make it fast and easy to add and change code. This saves programmers precious time and mental energy!

# BEHIND THE CODE

Computers do what we tell them to do. It may not be obvious at first what your code is instructing. But every line of code has a purpose!

Rectangles are built from four arguments insides parentheses. The argument values correspond to height and width of your **canvas** in pixels.

640px
x

360px y

The first and second arguments in the rect function indicate the distance in pixels from the left edge of the canvas and the distance in pixels from the top edge of the canvas.

```
6  var container2 = rect(220, 40, 110, 120);
```

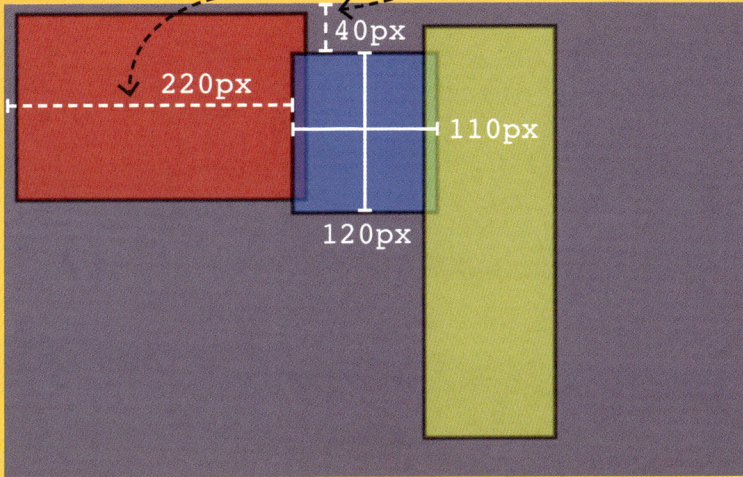

40px

220px

110px

120px

The third and fourth arguments in the rect function indicate the width of the rectangle in pixels and the height of the rectangle in pixels.

```
11  var container3 = rect(320, 20, 100, 310);
```

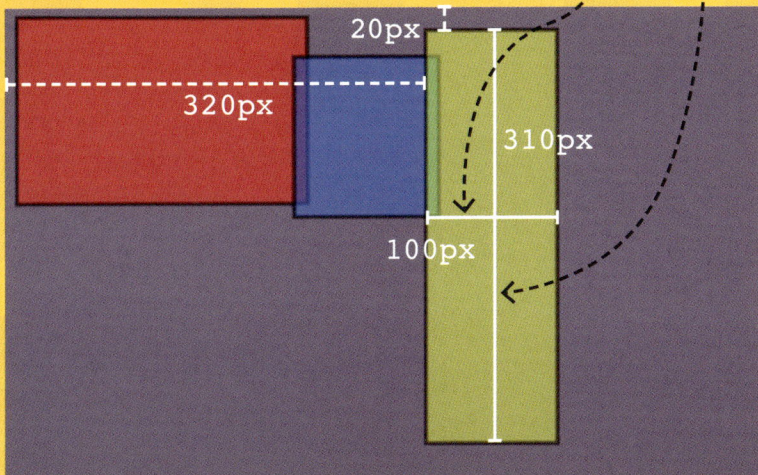

20px

320px

310px

100px

# DOODLE FILTER

Doodle on a video clip just as you would on paper! Use JavaScript's drawing function to enhance your video with a one-of-a-kind sketch.

## CODING SKILLS

- variables
- functions

1. Click on a video from Backgrounds.

2. From Effects, drag and drop the drawing block into the code editor.

3. Now use the cursor to draw directly on the video screen!

4. Change the drawing's properties, such as color, line width, and its 'x' and 'y' position by typing code directly into the code editor. Click through the Vidcode instructions for guidance on spelling and punctuation.

**1**

BACKGROUNDS  GRAPHICS  AUDIO

**3**

## HACK IT!
The order of arguments matters! The code `var my_drawing = drawing("blue", 10);` changes the drawing. But reversing the order of values to `(10, "blue")` does not.

**4**

```
 1  movie = video();
 2  movie.source = "anchor_1.mov";
 3
 4
 5  var my_drawing = drawing();
 6
 7  my_drawing.color = "yellow";
 8  my_drawing.lineWidth = 5;
 9
10  my_drawing.x = 300;
11  my_drawing.y = 10;
```

# FAMOUS FILTER

**PROJECT TIME:** 20 MINUTES

Have you ever used filter apps to enhance your photos? Create your very own filter with just a few lines of code!

Use **arrays** to store your filter values. An array is like a list with its items separated by commas. **Array index** tells us where to find it in the list. Programmers start counting from zero. So, the first value in an array is the zeroth item and has an array index of 0. The second value in an array has an array index of 1.

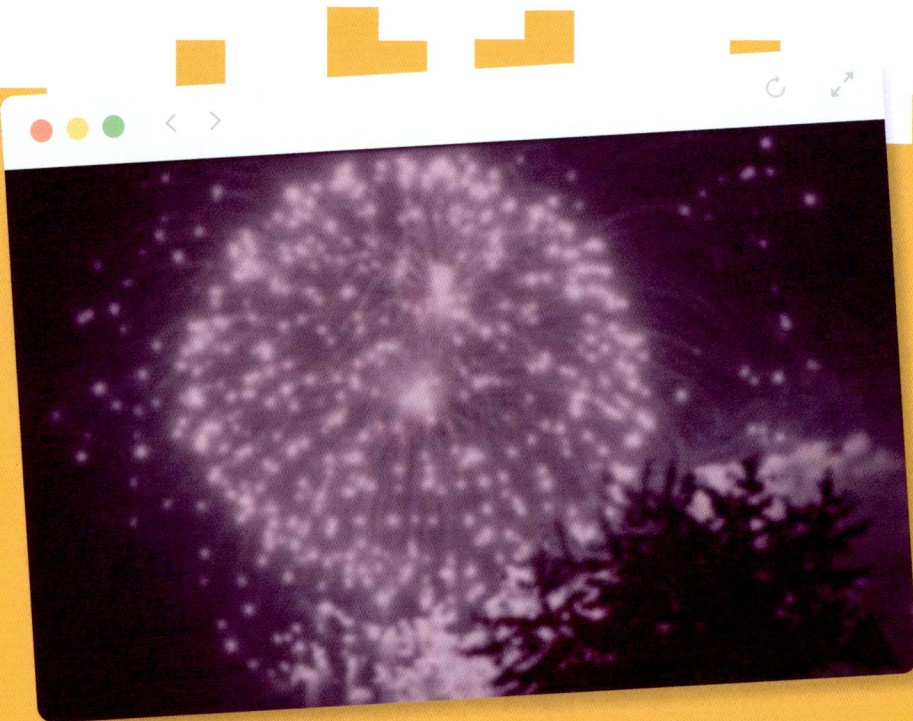

## CODING SKILLS
- variables
- arrays

1. Choose a video clip from Backgrounds or upload your own.

2. Drag and drop the blur, tint, and exposure blocks into the code editor in that order. Change the values of these properties until you get a filter that looks just right to you.

3. Above the lines of filter effects, type in this line of code:
```
var filter = [];
```

4. List the values of your filters inside the square brackets, in order, and separated by commas. The color value must be in quotations. Your array should look something like this, only with your own values:
```
var filter = [30, "orange", 40, 10];
```

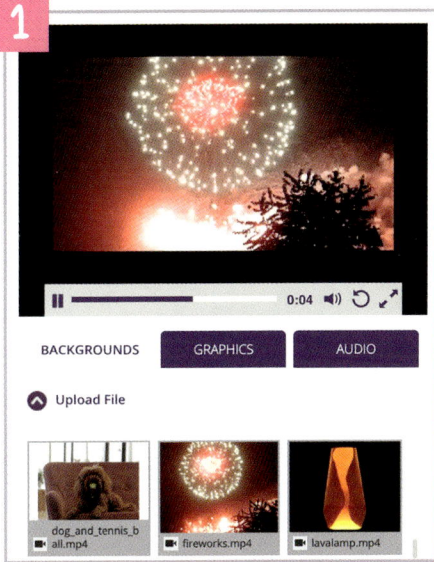

```
1  movie = video();
2  movie.source = "fireworks.mp4";
3
4  var filter =
5      [20, "purple", 40, 10];
6
7  blur(20);
8  tint("purple", 40);
9  exposure(10);
10
```

5. Now, instead of `blur(30);` you can use the array index to apply this filter. Change that line of code to:
`blur(filter[0]);`
The zero refers to the zeroth item in the array named filter.

6. Replace tint and exposure values using their array indexes too.

7. Give your filter a cool name. In the code editor, click on the code to change the word "filter" in `var filter =` to a new name you came up with.

8. Did the filter effect go away and stop working? Can you figure out why? You need to change the word "filter" to your cool name everywhere within the code! Do so and watch your filter effects return.

**6**
```
1 movie = video();
2 movie.source = "fireworks.mp4";
3
4 var filter = [20, "purple", 40, 10];
5
6 blur(filter[0]);
7 tint(filter[1], filter[2]);
8 exposure(filter[3]);
9
```

**8**
```
1 movie = video();
2 movie.source = "fireworks.mp4";
3
4 var amazing_filter = [20, "purple", 40, 10];
5
6 blur(amazing_filter[0]);
7 tint(amazing_filter[1], amazing_filter[2]);
8 exposure(amazing_filter[3]);
9
```

## CODING TIP!

A variable (`var` in JavaScript) can hold any type of value. This includes strings, numbers, arrays, even objects! Arrays are a handy way to store a bunch of items as a list, all inside one variable.

# TRUE COLORS

Design a flag using rectangles and circles!

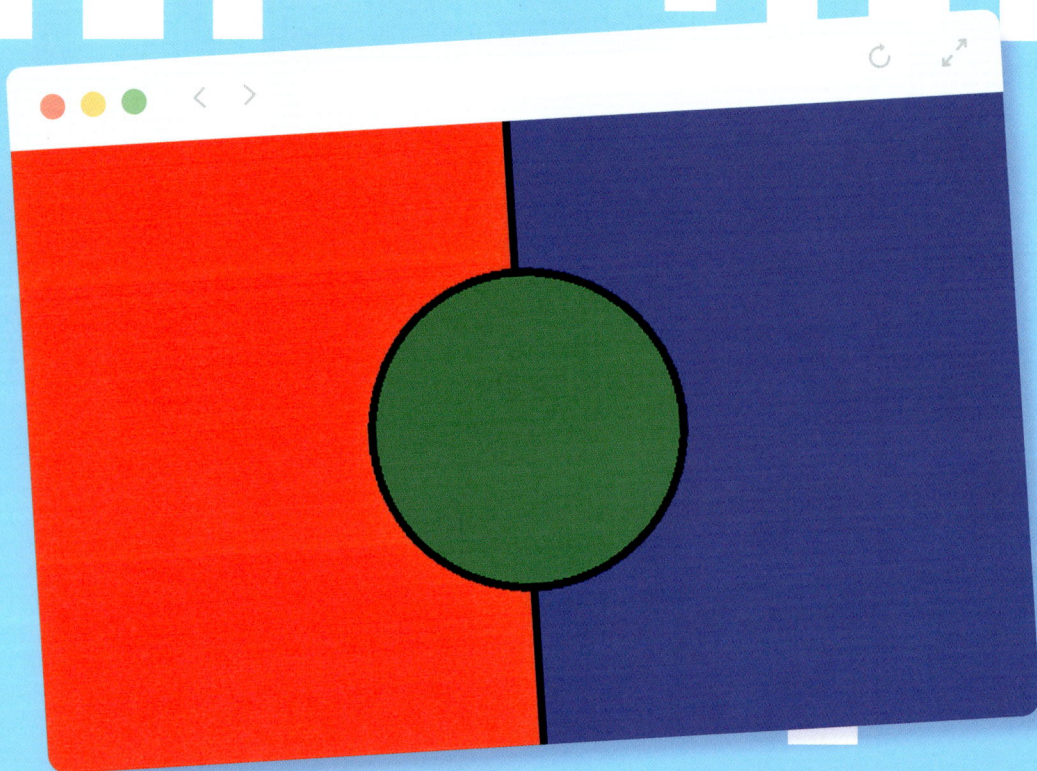

## CODING SKILLS

- variables
- arrays

1. In the code editor, type the line of code:
   `var flag_colors = [];`
   The brackets indicate an array. Arrays hold items in a list.

```
1 var flag_colors = [];
```

2. Type three colors inside the square brackets. Separate the colors with commas and enclose each color in quotations. You made an array!

```
1 var flag_colors =
2           ["red", "blue", "green"];
```

3. Later, we can use array index to refer to one of these colors. Remember, programmers start counting from zero. So, the first value in the array, red, is the zeroth item and has an array index of 0.

```
1 var flag_colors =
2           ["red", "blue", "green"];
3
4 var stripe_width = movie.width/2;
```

4. On a new line, type the code:
   `var stripe_width = movie.width/2;`
   This variable stores the code to make an object half the width of the canvas. Later, you can make a stripe for your flag that measures half the width of the canvas by referencing the variable name `stripe_width`.

## CODING TIP!
Variables and arrays can help you plan and organize information about width, height, and color.

5. On a new line, type the code:

   `var stripe_height = movie.height;`

   This variable stores the code to make an object the same height as the canvas. Later you can make a stripe for your flag that measures the same height as the canvas by referencing the variable name `stripe_height`.

6. Drag and drop a rectangle from the Effects tab into your code editor. This will be a stripe.

7. The function rect has four arguments listed in parentheses. These values refer to the 'x' position of the top left corner, the 'y' position of the top left corner, the rectangle's width, and the rectangle's height.

8. Reference the variable names from steps 4 and 5 to adjust the stripe's height and width.

9. Add a fifth value to the rect function to change the color of the stripe. Type `flag_colors[0]);` inside the parentheses, at the end of the array. Remember that the value 0 relates to the first color in the array from step 2.

**5**

```
1  var flag_colors =
2              ["red", "blue", "green"];
3
4  var stripe_width = movie.width/2;
5
6  var stripe_height = movie.height;
```

**6**

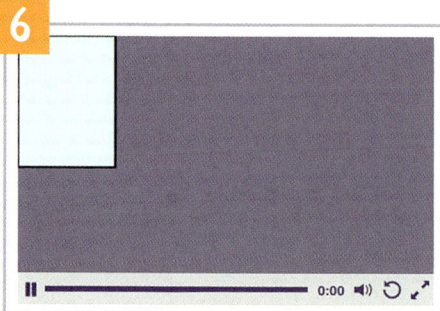

**8**

```
1  var flag_colors =
2              ["red", "blue", "green"];
3
4  var stripe_width = movie.width/2;
5
6  var stripe_height = movie.height;
7
8  var my_rect =
9    rect(0, 0, stripe_width, stripe_height);
```

**9**

```
1   var flag_colors =
2               ["red", "blue", "green"];
3
4   var stripe_width = movie.width/2;
5
6   var stripe_height = movie.height;
7
8   var my_rect =
9     rect(0, 0, stripe_width, stripe_height,
10            flag_colors[0]);
```

**10.** Change the value 0 to whichever number correlates to the color you want the stripe.

**11.** Repeat steps 6 through 8 to create a second stripe. Adjust the stripe's first, third, and fourth values to move it to the right side of the canvas:
```
var my_rect1 = rect
(movie.width/2, 0, stripe_
width, stripe_height);
```

**12.** Repeat steps 9 and 10 to change the second stripe's color.

**13.** Drag and drop a circle from the Effects tab into the code editor. Experiment with the circle's properties to position it how you like.

**14.** Add the argument
```
flag_colors[0]);
```
to the circle function arguments. Then, change the value to change the circle's color.

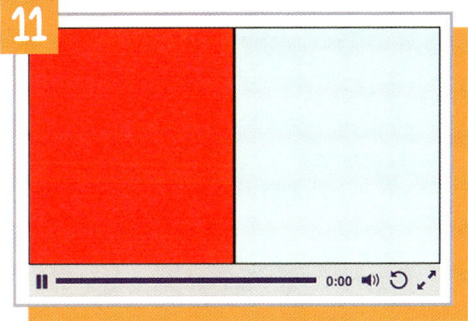

```
1  var flag_colors =
2          ["red", "blue", "green"];
3
4  var stripe_width = movie.width/2;
5
6  var stripe_height = movie.height;
7
8  var my_rect =
9    rect(0, 0, stripe_width, stripe_height,
10           flag_colors[0]);
11
12 var my_rect =
13    rect(movie.width/2, 0, stripe_width,
14           stripe_height, flag_colors[1]);
15
16 var my_circle = circle(320, 180, 100);
```

```
1  var flag_colors =
2          ["red", "blue", "green"];
3
4  var stripe_width = movie.width/2;
5
6  var stripe_height = movie.height;
7
8  var my_rect =
9    rect(0, 0, stripe_width, stripe_height,
10           flag_colors[0]);
11
12 var my_rect =
13    rect(movie.width/2, 0, stripe_width,
14           stripe_height, flag_colors[1]);
15
16 var my_circle =
17    circle(320, 180, 100, flag_colors[2]);
```

# SANDBOX FOR FREE CODING

Test your newfound skills and let your imagination guide your next fantastic filter!

## CODING SKILLS

- imagination
- exploration

1. Click on a video clip from the Backgrounds tab.

2. Mix, match, and experiment with filter options from the Effects tab.

3. Read through the Reference tab to see the different ways you can create cool coding projects with Vidcode. Cut and paste suggested snippets of code to see how it affects your work.

4. Click the "Save" button at the bottom of the code editor to save your project and come back to it later.

5. Click "Publish" to put your new project online for others to admire!

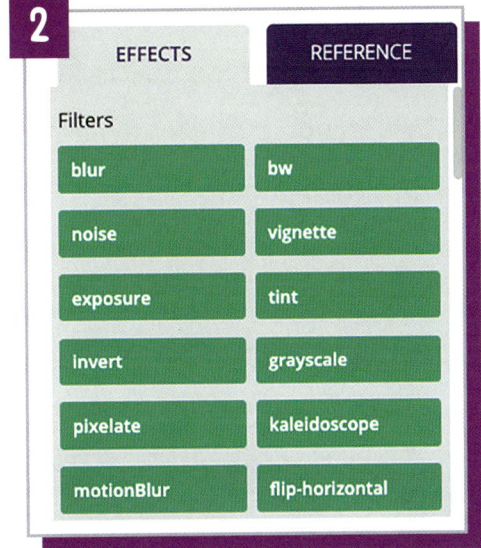

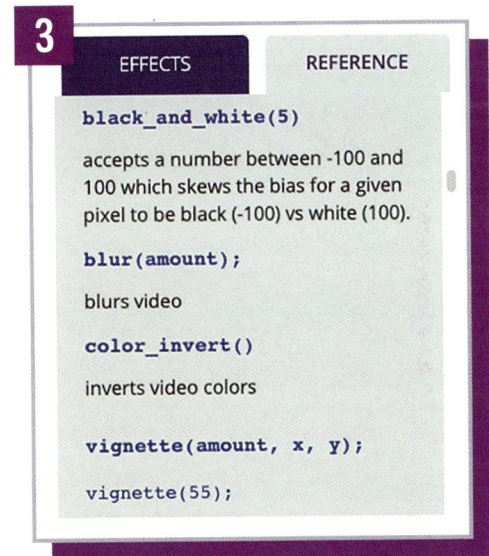

**2**

| EFFECTS | REFERENCE |
|---------|-----------|

Filters

| blur | bw |
|------|-----|
| noise | vignette |
| exposure | tint |
| invert | grayscale |
| pixelate | kaleidoscope |
| motionBlur | flip-horizontal |

**3**

| EFFECTS | REFERENCE |
|---------|-----------|

```
black_and_white(5)
```

accepts a number between -100 and 100 which skews the bias for a given pixel to be black (-100) vs white (100).

```
blur(amount);
```

blurs video

```
color_invert()
```

inverts video colors

```
vignette(amount, x, y);

vignette(55);
```

## CODING TIP!

Imagination is essential to becoming an expert coder. Have fun coding and creating awesome projects to share with friends and family!

# CONCLUSION

You are a coder who can now speak JavaScript! Take your skills to the next level by working on the Vidcode platform to continue learning by doing.

Have fun making awesome coding projects!

## MORE ABOUT VIDCODE

Vidcode is a coding platform and curriculum that teaches computer science, object oriented programming, web programming, design, & JavaScript. The magic behind Vidcode has an academic term—computational media! This means learners can upload photos, illustrations, videos and audio—and manipulate them with code right away, allowing tweens and teens to connect computer programming to the media they interact with every day. Vidcode was founded by three women—an engineer, an educator, and an artist. We're now a global team that supports schools, libraries and individual learners in leveraging our 300+ hours of online coding tutorials.

**Visit www.vidcode.com for more information.**

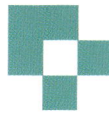

# GLOSSARY

**argument:** a specific value that acts as input to a function

**array:** a list of values

**array index:** a number that tells you where an item is in an array

**canvas:** the top-right screen in Vidcode where your coding is displayed as pictures

**code editor:** the white box where your code is written

**coding:** writing instructions for a computer. Computer programs are coded.

**data types:** strings or numbers are examples of data types. They indicate the type of information a computer program processes.

**function:** a set of instructions to do a specific task

**object:** a container or an entity

**opacity:** the measure of how see-through something is

**pixel:** a square of color on a computer screen. Images can be made up of thousands of pixels.

**program:** a specific set of ordered commands for a computer to perform. To program is to write these commands.

**programming language:** a set of words and rules for giving instructions that a computer understands

**property:** a value that belongs to an object

**sequence:** the order in which the commands are executed by a computer

**string:** a collection of text, punctuation, and spaces

**value:** data such as numbers or text that can be manipulated by a computer program

**variable:** a container that can store a value

# INDEX

# PHOTO ACKNOWLEDGMENTS

The images in this book are used with the permission of: © FatCamera/iStockphoto, pp. 15, 23; © FG Trade/iStockphoto, p. 30; © fizkes/iStockphoto, p. 28 (girl); © monkeybusinessimages/iStockphoto, p. 4 (boy); © vgajic/iStockphoto, p. 5; © Vidcode/Mighty Media, Inc., pp. 4, 6, 7, 8, 9, 10, 11, 12, 13, 14, 16, 17, 18, 19, 20, 21, 22, 24, 25, 26, 27, 28, 29.

Cover Photos: © fizkes/iStockphoto; © Vidcode/Mighty Media, Inc.

Design Elements: © Alexey Bezrodny/iStockphoto (arrow); © artishokcs/iStockphoto (pixel background); © filborg/iStockphoto (browser window); © Mighty Media, Inc. (blocks)

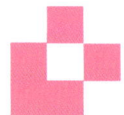